Birds on a Wire

Birds ON A Wire

A Renga 'Round Town

J. Patrick Lewis
Paul B. Janeczko

ILLUSTRATIONS BY
Gary Lippincott

WORDSONG
Honesdale, Pennsylvania

For Paula, Gayle, and Roberta.
Love, Pat

For Tammy Begin-LeBlanc and Richard Pollock,
who listened without judging.
Always, Paul

To Patience.
Gary

Text copyright © 2008 by J. Patrick Lewis and Paul B. Janeczko
Illustrations copyright © 2008 by Gary Lippincott
All rights reserved
Printed in China
Designed by Helen Robinson
First edition

LIBRARY OF CONGRESS CATALOGING-IN-PUBLICATION DATA
Lewis, J. Patrick.
Birds on a wire : a Renga 'round town / J. Patrick Lewis & Paul B. Janeczko ;
illustrations by Gary Lippincott.
p. cm.
ISBN-13: 978-1-59078-383-2 (hardcover : alk. paper)
1. Children's poetry, American. 2. Renga, American. I. Janeczko, Paul B.
II. Lippincott, Gary A., ill. III. Title.
PS3562.E9465B57 2008
811'.54—dc22   2006011582

WORDSONG
An Imprint of Boyds Mills Press, Inc.
815 Church Street
Honesdale, Pennsylvania 18431

Introduction

What, you might be wondering, is a renga? Like a haiku, a renga is an ancient Japanese verse form in which poets take turns adding verses. The word is both singular and plural, like *sheep* or *salmon*. A renga (meaning "linked verse") isn't nearly as well known as a haiku, and that's too bad because haiku really evolved from renga.

A traditional renga is written by two or more poets. The first poet writes three lines (similar to a haiku), the second poet follows that with two lines, the first poet comes back with another three lines, then two, three, two, and so on. Like railroad cars in a line, each verse links in some way with the one preceding it, but not with the others. That means that each new verse can send you off in a completely different direction. And the next poet must discover how to connect to the new verse. By the way, *Birds on a Wire* is untraditional. We each wrote five lines and broke them into three-line and two-line stanzas.

How long is a renga? That's up to you. It can be a hundred verses or more. But even though a renga doesn't actually tell a story, it should have a beginning, a middle, and an end.

We don't want to bore you with all the rules for rengas. The important thing to remember is that this is an exciting new—but really old, about eight hundred years old!—way of creating poems for two (or more) voices. Why not get together with a couple of your friends and see if you can create a renga of your own. You just might get hooked on this wonderful Japanese-style verse.

J.P.L. and P.B.J.

in the blizzard
of apple blossoms,
a road edged in white

old spotted hound
stops to sniff

flood waters on the creek!
bon voyage, grasshopper,
on this morning's paper boat

carrying news
to nowhere

in yellow boots
the florist mists pails
of daffodils

*her sidewalk the only one
with rainbows in the noon sun*

munching on sugar doughnuts
from The Chocolatéclair
two boys stop suddenly

amazed that morning ends
in a pot of gold

glazed with rain
a red wheelbarrow headstands
by the hardware store

*the old doctor recalls
childhood barnyard*

two blocks beyond excitement,
the town's tiny Ferris wheel
twenty years dead-still

circling him back to a girl
twirling through the sky

at the ballpark
bees roam the outfield
clover to clover

in the empty dugout
a pigeon rides the bench

ambulance wails
behind a motorcycle parade
of one

*always something
to spoil the moment*

behind their teacher
a line of first-graders
each clutching a new book

crossing at the **WALK** *sign*
make way for readers

"How's the good Dr. Darigan?"
"Did you hear? The librarian …"
"No, I wouldn't tell a soul."

nothing quite as American
as small-town gossip

beauty salon women
study grandchildren photos
each knows the cutest

with hair sprayed and fixed, they leave
proud to show off the natural look

purses fall open
car keys jangle
the busyness of life

no one is watching
the hemlocks snowing

the small black eyes
of the trembling mouse
mark the hawk's circle

dash to stone-wall sanctuary
proves timing is everything

a moveable feast
but sky shadows mapping the town
cease in the aerie air

delay not defeat
proves patience is virtue

basketball taps
its message on playground—then
silence before *swish*

*shouts and yelps of kids
giants in their dreams*

a hummingbird plays
its own game
homing in curious

to kiss Miss DiPietro's
ruby red lipstick

spinning Frisbee flies
straight and true, hits a snag
leaping mutt's teeth

others watch the hot-dog vendor
hoping for a pickup snack

the afternoon turns
shades of mustard
four-leggeds step back

cocking their heads
good breeding, thinks the widow

ring worn smooth with age
hands clutch knob of her cane
cool under the scarlet awning

she stares in dress-shop window
wondering who would wear that

"Here comes Sunshine"
the mayor's syrupy greeting
she grumbles out loud

*Everything is going
out of fashion*

in white window box
a violet tangle:
petunias rioting

old spotted hound doesn't notice
as he passes, head down

but there, right there
a crack in the sidewalk
new five-dollar bill

poor dog ignores it
money can't buy you love

paperboy trudges
door-to-door bringing news
heavy on his shoulder

then homeward on sidewalk and street
knowing no news is good news

browned-around creamed corn
pigs in a blanket, pecan pie
Mother magic

dinner sweetened
with grapes of talk

birds on a wire
in failing light turn home
to oak and elm

park trees become noisemakers
until the flock of screeches stills

velveteen hush of evening
purples willow marsh
cicada chatter

burglar-night steals
a jewel tray of stars